I0017324

The Ultimate Guide to Creating a Website with Hostinger

Build, Optimize & Launch Your Website – No Coding Required!

Introduction

In today's digital world, having a website is essential for businesses, bloggers, and professionals alike. Whether you want to launch an e-commerce store, create a personal blog, or establish an online presence for your brand, **Hostinger** offers an affordable and user-friendly solution.

This **comprehensive guide** will walk you through the entire website creation process, from **domain registration** to **website optimization**, ensuring that your site is fast, secure, and SEO-friendly.

Why Choose Hostinger for Website Creation?

Hostinger is one of the leading web hosting providers, known for its **affordable pricing, fast-loading servers**, and **easy-to-use control panel**. Here's why it stands out:

- **Budget-Friendly Plans:** Suitable for beginners and businesses of all sizes.
- **User-Friendly Interface:** Intuitive dashboard and one-click website setup.
- **High-Performance Hosting:** SSD storage, LiteSpeed servers, and global data centers.

- **Free Domain & SSL:** Secure your website with HTTPS for better SEO rankings.
- **24/7 Customer Support:** Reliable assistance whenever you need it.

What You'll Learn in This Guide

By the end of this tutorial, you'll have a fully functional website with Hostinger. Here's a sneak peek at what we'll cover:

1. **Registering a Domain Name** – Choosing the perfect domain for your website.
2. **Setting Up Hosting** – Selecting the right Hostinger plan and configuring your hosting account.
3. **Installing WordPress (or Another CMS)** – A step-by-step guide to installing and setting up your website.
4. **Customizing Your Website** – Selecting a theme, adding essential plugins, and designing pages.
5. **Optimizing for Speed & Security** – Ensuring your website is fast and protected from cyber threats.
6. **SEO Best Practices** – Improving your website's visibility on Google and other search engines.
7. **Launching & Managing Your Website** – Final steps to go live and maintain your site.

Whether you're a **beginner** or have some **experience with web development**, this guide will provide **actionable insights** to help you launch a successful website on Hostinger.

Let's get started!

Chapter 1: Understanding Hostinger and Its Benefits

Creating a website starts with choosing the right hosting provider, and **Hostinger** has established itself as a reliable and affordable solution for individuals and businesses alike. Whether you are launching a personal blog, an e-commerce store, or a professional portfolio, understanding how Hostinger works and what it offers will help you make an informed decision.

In this chapter, we will explore what Hostinger is, its key features, and how to select the right hosting plan based on your needs.

1.1 What is Hostinger?

Overview of Hostinger's Hosting Services

Hostinger is a globally recognized web hosting company that provides **affordable, high-performance hosting solutions** for individuals, small businesses, and developers. Established in 2004, it has grown to serve millions of users worldwide. Hostinger offers a range of hosting options, including:

- **Shared Hosting** – A budget-friendly solution for beginners.
- **VPS Hosting** – A more powerful and flexible option for growing websites.
- **Cloud Hosting** – Ideal for businesses that need scalability and high performance.
- **WordPress Hosting** – Optimized for WordPress users with fast-loading speeds.

- **E-commerce Hosting** – Tailored for online stores, with WooCommerce support.

Why Choose Hostinger Over Competitors?

There are numerous web hosting providers on the market, but Hostinger stands out due to its combination of **affordability, reliability, and user-friendly experience**. Here's why many users prefer Hostinger over competitors like Bluehost, SiteGround, or GoDaddy:

- **Competitive Pricing** – Hostinger offers some of the lowest hosting prices without compromising on performance.

- **Fast Loading Times** – Thanks to **LiteSpeed servers** and **SSD storage**, Hostinger provides **faster website speeds** compared to many shared hosting providers.

- **Global Data Centers** – Hostinger operates **multiple data centers worldwide**, ensuring low latency and **better website performance** in different regions.

- **Intuitive hPanel** – Unlike the traditional cPanel, Hostinger's custom-built **hPanel** offers a **modern, user-friendly interface** for website management.

- **Excellent Security Features** – Free **SSL certificates, automated backups, malware scanning**, and **DDoS protection** help keep your website safe.

- **24/7 Customer Support** – Hostinger provides **round-the-clock support via live chat**, ensuring you get help whenever needed.

- Optimized for WordPress – With **one-click WordPress installation**, pre-installed caching, and automatic updates, Hostinger is a great choice for WordPress users.

If you are looking for a **cost-effective, fast, and beginner-friendly hosting provider**, Hostinger is one of the best choices available.

1.2 Key Features of Hostinger

1-Affordable Pricing

Hostinger is known for its **budget-friendly pricing**, with plans starting as low as **$1.99 per month**. Unlike many hosting providers that charge extra for essential features, Hostinger includes a **free domain, SSL certificate, and email hosting** in most plans.

2-Free Domain & SSL

- When you sign up for a **Premium** or **Business** hosting plan, you get a **free domain name** for the first year.
- Hostinger includes a **free SSL certificate**, ensuring your website is secure and ranks higher on search engines.

3-User-Friendly Control Panel (hPanel)

- Unlike traditional **cPanel**, Hostinger's **hPanel** is **more modern and beginner-friendly**.
- Easily **manage domains, install applications, set up email accounts, and monitor performance** from a single dashboard.

4-Fast Performance & Uptime

- Hostinger uses **LiteSpeed Web Server technology** for **optimized loading speeds**.
- With an average uptime of **99.9%**, your website remains online with minimal downtime.
- **Global CDN integration** further improves website speed for visitors worldwide.

5-24/7 Customer Support

- Hostinger provides **24/7 live chat support** in multiple languages.
- Their knowledge base and step-by-step tutorials help beginners resolve common issues quickly.

1.3 Choosing the Right Hosting Plan

Selecting the best **Hostinger hosting plan** depends on your **website type, traffic expectations, and technical expertise**. Let's break down the available options and their use cases.

1Shared Hosting: Best for Beginners

Overview:
Shared hosting means **multiple websites share the same server resources**. It's the **most affordable and beginner-friendly** option.

Best For:
- Personal blogs, portfolios, and small business websites.
- Those on a **tight budget**.
- Beginners with **no technical experience**.

Pros:
Low cost (starting at **$1.99/month**).
Easy setup with **one-click WordPress installation**.
Free domain & SSL included.

Cons:
X Shared resources can affect performance if other websites on the server consume too much bandwidth.
X Limited scalability – not ideal for high-traffic sites.

2-VPS Hosting: Best for Growing Websites & Developers

Overview:
VPS (Virtual Private Server) hosting provides **dedicated resources** within a shared environment, offering **better performance and flexibility**.

Best For:
- Websites expecting **higher traffic**.
- Developers who need **custom server configurations**.
- Businesses running **web applications** or e-commerce stores.

Pros:
More **server control and customization** than shared hosting.
Better performance & scalability.
Dedicated resources prevent slowdowns.

Cons:
X Higher cost than shared hosting (starting at **$3.99/month**).
X Requires **some technical knowledge** to manage.

3-Cloud Hosting: Best for High-Performance & Large Businesses

Overview:
Cloud hosting distributes your website across **multiple interconnected servers**, ensuring **high availability, redundancy, and scalability**.

Best For:
- Large-scale businesses, e-commerce stores, and high-traffic websites.
- Those who need **near-zero downtime** and **lightning-fast performance**.

Pros:
Auto-scaling resources – Handles traffic spikes effortlessly.
Better security and redundancy.
Faster speeds with **dedicated resources**.

Cons:
X More expensive than shared and VPS hosting (starting at **$9.99/month**).
X Requires **technical knowledge** to fully utilize advanced features.

Which Hosting Plan is Right for You?

Hosting Type	Best For	Price Range	Technical Knowledge Required
Shared Hosting	Beginners, personal blogs, small businesses	$1.99–$4.99/month	Beginner-friendly
VPS Hosting	Developers, growing businesses, custom applications	$3.99–$38.99/month	Intermediate
Cloud Hosting	Large-scale websites, e-commerce stores	$9.99–$69.99/month	Advanced

Final Thoughts

Choosing the **right Hostinger plan** is crucial for your website's performance and scalability. If you're just starting, **Shared Hosting** is the best option. If you expect **higher traffic** or need **more control**, consider **VPS or Cloud Hosting**.

With its **affordable pricing, fast performance, and excellent support**, Hostinger is an **ideal choice for website owners of all levels**.

Chapter 2: Registering a Domain Name

A domain name is **your website's identity on the internet**, making it one of the most critical aspects of building an online presence. Choosing the **right domain name** impacts your **brand credibility, SEO ranking, and user trust**.

In this chapter, we will guide you through **how to choose an SEO-friendly domain, check availability, and register it on Hostinger step by step**.

2.1 How to Choose a Domain Name

Your domain name is the **first impression** users and search engines get about your website. Choosing a **memorable, relevant, and SEO-optimized** domain can boost your website's visibility and traffic.

Best Practices for an SEO-Friendly Domain Name

- **Keep It Short & Simple**

  - Aim for **10-15 characters** for easy recall (e.g., **TechGuru.com**).
  - Avoid long, complicated names that are hard to remember.

- **Use Keywords Strategically**

  - If possible, include a **keyword relevant to your niche** (e.g., **BestYogaTips.com** for a yoga blog).

- Avoid keyword stuffing, which can look spammy (**Bad Example: CheapBestYogaDiscount.com**).

- Choose a Brandable Name

- A unique, **brandable** domain (e.g., **Apple.com, Zillow.com**) is **more memorable** than generic names.
- Avoid **hyphens** and **numbers**, which can be confusing (**Bad Example: Best-Yoga-Tips123.com**).

- Pick the Right Domain Extension (.com, .net, .org, etc.)

- **.com** is the most **trusted and widely recognized** extension.
- **.net** and **.org** are good alternatives if **.com is unavailable**.
- For local businesses, consider **country-specific extensions** (e.g., **.co.uk, .ca, .de**).

- Avoid Copyright & Trademark Issues

- **Double-check** that your domain isn't infringing on **existing brand names**.
- Use tools like **USPTO (United States Patent and Trademark Office)** to ensure compliance.

Checking Domain Availability

Before registering a domain, you need to **verify its availability**. Here's how:

1 Use Hostinger's Domain Checker

- Go to **Hostinger's Domain Search**.
- Enter your desired domain name and check for availability.

2-Check Alternative Suggestions

- If your preferred domain is **taken**, Hostinger will **suggest variations**.
- Try adding a **short prefix or suffix** (e.g., **MyTechGuru.com** instead of **TechGuru.com**).

3-Verify Social Media Availability

- Ensure your **brand name** is available on **social media platforms** (e.g., Twitter, Instagram, Facebook).
- Tools like **Namechk.com** can help check social handle availability.

2.2 Registering Your Domain on Hostinger

Once you've chosen a domain name, follow these **simple steps** to **register it on Hostinger**.

Step-by-Step Guide to Purchasing a Domain

1Visit Hostinger's Domain Registration Page

- Go to **https://www.hostinger.com**.
- Click on **"Domains"** in the navigation menu.

2-Search for Your Desired Domain

- Type your domain name into the search bar.
- If available, click **"Add to Cart"**.
- If unavailable, select a suggested alternative or try a new search.

3-Choose a Registration Period

- Domains are available for **1, 2, 3, or 5 years**.
- Longer registration can help with **SEO and branding consistency**.

4-Enable Domain Privacy Protection (Recommended)

- **Domain privacy protection** hides your **personal information** from public WHOIS records.
- Prevents spam, identity theft, and unwanted marketing emails.
- **Highly recommended** for all website owners.

5-Proceed to Checkout

- Click **"Continue to Cart"**.
- If you haven't already, create a **Hostinger account** or log in.
- Choose a **payment method** (Credit Card, PayPal, Google Pay, etc.).

6-Complete Your Purchase

- Review your order and click **"Submit Payment"**.
- You will receive an **email confirmation** once the purchase is successful.

Setting Up Domain Privacy Protection

By default, all domain registrations are stored in a public **WHOIS database**, showing your **name, email, phone number, and address**. To protect your privacy, **enable WHOIS Privacy Protection**.

Steps to Enable Domain Privacy on Hostinger

1Go to Hostinger's Dashboard (hPanel)

- Log in to your **Hostinger account**.
- Navigate to **"Domains"** → Select your purchased domain.

2-Activate WHOIS Privacy Protection

- Find the option for **Privacy Protection**.
- Click **"Enable"** and confirm the activation.

3-Verify the Changes

- Visit a **WHOIS lookup tool** (e.g., **who.is**).
- Search for your domain to check if your details are hidden.

Benefits of Privacy Protection:
- Prevents **spam emails and telemarketing**.
- Protects against **identity theft** and **domain hijacking**.
- Keeps your **personal information private** from competitors.

Registering the **right domain name** is the first step toward building a successful website. By **choosing an SEO-friendly name, checking its availability, and enabling domain privacy protection**, you lay the foundation for a **strong online presence**.

3.2 Connecting Your Domain to Hosting

Once you've **purchased a hosting plan**, the next step is to **connect your domain** so visitors can access your website.

Updating Nameservers on Hostinger

Nameservers link your domain to your web hosting. Hostinger's default nameservers are:

. **ns1.dns-parking.com**
. **ns2.dns-parking.com**

How to Update Nameservers on Hostinger

1Log in to Your Hostinger Dashboard

- Go to **Hostinger hPanel** and log in.
- Click on **"Domains"** and select your registered domain.

2-Change the Nameservers

- Navigate to **"DNS / Nameservers"**.
- Replace the existing nameservers with:

```
CopierModifier
ns1.dns-parking.com
ns2.dns-parking.com
```

- Click **Save Changes**.

3-Verify & Wait for Propagation

- Domain propagation takes **up to 24 hours** to update worldwide.
- Use **DNS Checker** (https://dnschecker.org/) to confirm changes.

Understanding DNS Settings

Once your domain is connected, you can modify DNS records to control how your domain interacts with your hosting:

DNS Record	Function
A Record	Links your domain to an IP address
CNAME Record	Redirects a subdomain to another domain
MX Record	Manages email services

 Tip: If you're using **Google Workspace or Zoho Mail** for emails, update the **MX Records** in Hostinger's hPanel.

3.3 Accessing Hostinger's hPanel

Hostinger uses **hPanel**, a user-friendly control panel to manage websites, domains, databases, and security settings.

Overview of the hPanel Dashboard

After logging into **Hostinger hPanel**, you'll find:

. **Hosting** – Manage website files, databases, security, and PHP settings.
. **Domains** – Configure DNS, nameservers, and SSL certificates.
. **Email** – Set up business emails (e.g., **yourname@yourdomain.com**).
. **Website Builder** – Install WordPress or use Hostinger's drag-and-drop builder.
. **Files Manager** – Upload, edit, and manage website files.

Managing Hosting Settings

1Installing WordPress

- Navigate to **Website → Auto Installer**.
- Select **WordPress**, enter admin details, and install.

2-Adding SSL for Security

- Go to **SSL → Manage SSL Certificates**.
- Click **"Install"** to activate **free SSL encryption**.

3-Setting Up Backups

- Under **Files → Backups**, schedule **automatic backups** to protect your data.

Final Thoughts

Now that your **domain is connected, and your hosting is set up**, you're ready to start **building your website!**

Chapter 4: Installing and Configuring WordPress

WordPress powers **over 40% of websites worldwide**, making it the **most popular content management system (CMS)**. It's **flexible, user-friendly, and highly customizable**, making it perfect for **blogs, business websites, e-commerce stores, and portfolios**.

In this chapter, you'll learn how to:
- Install WordPress **quickly** using Hostinger's **Auto-Installer**
- Configure **essential WordPress settings** for performance & SEO
- Optimize permalinks and basic site settings

Let's get started!

4.1 Why Use WordPress?

Before installing WordPress, let's explore **why it's the best choice** for your website.

Advantages of WordPress

- **Beginner-Friendly** – No coding knowledge required
- **Highly Customizable** – Thousands of themes & plugins
- **SEO Optimized** – Built-in SEO features for better Google rankings
- **Fast & Scalable** – Works well for small blogs to large businesses
- **Secure & Regularly Updated** – Constant improvements & security patches

WordPress vs. Other Website Builders

Feature	WordPress	Wix	Squarespace	Shopify (for eCommerce)
Customization	- Full control	X Limited	X Limited	X Limited
SEO-Friendly	- Excellent	X Basic	X Basic	X Limited
Cost-Effective	- Free (Hosting Required)	X Monthly Fees	X Monthly Fees	X Transaction Fees
Plugins & Add-ons	- 60,000+	X Limited	X Limited	X Limited
E-commerce Support	- WooCommerce	X Limited	X Limited	- Built-in

 Best For: WordPress is the #1 choice for flexibility, cost-effectiveness, and long-term scalability.

4.2 One-Click WordPress Installation

Hostinger makes installing WordPress **super easy** with its **Auto-Installer**.

How to Install WordPress via Hostinger's Auto-Installer

1 **Log in to Hostinger hPanel**

- Go to **https://www.hostinger.com/cpanel-login** and sign in.

2- **Navigate to Auto-Installer**

- Click **"Website"** → **"Auto Installer"**
- Select **WordPress**

3-Enter Your Website Details

- **Website URL**: Choose **yourdomain.com** or www.yourdomain.com
- **Administrator Email**: Use a strong, secure email
- **Admin Username & Password**: Create a **secure login** (avoid "admin" as the username)
- **Website Title**: Enter your **brand name** or **blog name**
- **Language**: Select your preferred language

4-Select Database Configuration

- Keep **default settings** unless you need custom database options

5-Click "Install"

- WordPress installation takes **less than a minute**!

6-Log in to Your WordPress Dashboard

- Go to **yourdomain.com/wp-admin**
- Enter your **admin credentials** and **log in**

Congratulations! You now have **WordPress installed** on your website.

4.3 Configuring Basic WordPress Settings

Now that WordPress is installed, let's **configure the essential settings** for a **fast, SEO-friendly, and user-friendly website**.

1Setting Up Website Title & Tagline

Your **website title** appears in search results and browser tabs. The **tagline** is a short description of your website.

. **Go to: Settings → General**
. **Enter Your Site Title & Tagline**
. Click **"Save Changes"**

 SEO Tip: Use a **keyword-rich tagline** like:
- **"Best Digital Marketing Tips for Entrepreneurs"** instead of
"Just another WordPress site"

2-Managing Permalinks for SEO

Permalinks define **how your URLs look**. For example:
X **yourdomain.com/?p=123** (Bad for SEO)
- **yourdomain.com/best-seo-tips/** (Good for SEO)

. **Go to: Settings → Permalinks**
. Select **"Post Name"**
. Click **"Save Changes"**

Why? "Post Name" is **clean, readable, and helps SEO.**

3-Setting Up Your Homepage

. **Go to: Settings → Reading**
. Choose:

- **Static Page** (for business websites, portfolios)
- **Latest Posts** (for blogs)
  - . Click **"Save Changes"**

4-Enabling SSL for Security

SSL (Secure Socket Layer) protects your website by enabling **HTTPS encryption**.

. **Go to: Hostinger hPanel → SSL → Install Free SSL**
. Enable **HTTPS Redirect**

- Your site is now **secure**.

5-Setting Up Site Language & Timezone

. **Go to: Settings → General**
. Select **your preferred language & timezone**
. Click **"Save Changes"**

- This ensures **correct timestamps** for blog posts & scheduling.

6-Installing Essential Plugins

. **Go to: Plugins → Add New**
. Install & Activate the following:

- **SEO: Yoast SEO** or **Rank Math** (for better Google rankings)
- **Security: Wordfence** (protects from hackers)
- **Backup: UpdraftPlus** (creates automatic backups)
- **Performance: WP Rocket** (improves website speed)

 Bonus Tip: Only install **essential** plugins to keep your site **fast & lightweight**.

Final Thoughts

You did it! Your WordPress site is now installed & configured!

Chapter 5: Choosing and Customizing a Theme

Your website's theme **determines its design, layout, and overall user experience**. Choosing the right theme is crucial for **SEO, speed, and branding**.

In this chapter, we'll cover:
- How to **select the best WordPress theme** for your needs
- How to **customize your theme** with colors, fonts, and logos
- Must-have **plugins** for SEO, security, and performance

Let's dive in!

5.1 Selecting the Right Theme

WordPress offers **over 10,000 free and premium themes**, but not all are **fast, SEO-friendly, and mobile-responsive**.

Free vs. Premium Themes: Which One to Choose?

Feature	Free Themes	Premium Themes
Cost	- Free	X Paid ($30-$100)
Customization	X Limited options	- Full control
Support & Updates	X Community-based	- Dedicated support
SEO & Speed	- Some are optimized	- Often highly optimized
Security	X Can be vulnerable	- Regular updates

Recommendation:
If you're just starting out, try **a free, lightweight theme** like

Astra or **GeneratePress**.
 If you want advanced design & performance, **invest in a premium theme** like **Kadence, OceanWP, or Blocksy**.

Best WordPress Themes for SEO & Performance

. **Astra** – Fast, lightweight, and highly customizable (Great for blogs & businesses)
. **GeneratePress** – Minimalist & super-fast (Best for performance-focused websites)
. **Kadence** – Powerful, feature-rich, and beginner-friendly
. **OceanWP** – Perfect for e-commerce & multipurpose sites
. **Neve** – Mobile-first & AMP-ready for fast loading

- **All these themes** are **SEO-friendly, responsive, and optimized for speed**.

5.2 Customizing Your Theme

After selecting a theme, it's time to **customize your website's look** using **WordPress Customizer**.

How to Access the WordPress Customizer

1Go to **Appearance → Themes → Customize**
2-You'll see a **live preview** of your website
3-Customize the following:

1Adding Your Logo & Site Identity

. **Go to: Appearance → Customize → Site Identity**
. Upload your **logo** (PNG/SVG format)
. Set your **Site Title & Tagline**

- **SEO Tip:** Your **Site Title** should include **your main keyword** (e.g., "Best Travel Blog for Digital Nomads")

2-Choosing Colors & Fonts

. **Go to: Appearance → Customize → Colors**
. Pick a **color scheme that matches your brand**

. **Go to: Appearance → Customize → Typography**
. Select **Google Fonts** (use readable fonts like Poppins, Lato, or Open Sans)

Tip:
Dark text on a light background improves readability.
Avoid using too many colors—stick to **2-3 brand colors.**

3-Setting Up a Homepage Layout

. **Go to: Settings → Reading**
. Choose:

- **Static Page** (For business websites)
- **Latest Posts** (For blogs)

- **SEO Tip:** Use **an engaging homepage with a strong call-to-action (CTA).**

4-Customizing the Header & Footer

. **Go to: Appearance → Customize → Header/Footer**
. Add **menu links, social icons, and contact details**
. Use a **sticky header** (so navigation stays visible while scrolling)

- **User Experience Tip:** Keep menus **simple**—limit to **5-6 main pages**.

5-Optimizing for Mobile & Responsiveness

. **Go to: Appearance → Customize → Responsive View**
. Test your site on **desktop, tablet, and mobile**
. Adjust **font sizes, buttons, and spacing**

 Google Prioritizes Mobile-Friendly Websites—make sure **your theme is responsive!**

5.3 Installing Essential Plugins

Plugins **add extra functionality** to your WordPress site. Here are the **must-have plugins** for SEO, security, and speed.

1SEO Plugins (For Better Google Rankings)

- **Yoast SEO** – Helps optimize pages, meta titles, and XML sitemaps
- **Rank Math** – Powerful, beginner-friendly SEO plugin
- **All in One SEO** – A solid alternative for optimizing posts & pages

 Bonus Tip: Configure **meta descriptions & alt texts** for images to **boost SEO**.

2-Security Plugins (To Protect Your Website)

- **Wordfence** – Blocks malware & hackers
- **Sucuri** – Monitors website security & removes threats
- **iThemes Security** – Strengthens login security

- **Pro Tip:** Enable **Two-Factor Authentication (2FA)** for admin logins!

3-Performance Optimization Plugins (For Faster Loading Times)

- **WP Rocket** – The best caching plugin (improves site speed)
- **LiteSpeed Cache** – Works great with Hostinger's LiteSpeed servers
- **Smush** – Compresses images to make your site load faster
- **Autoptimize** – Optimizes CSS & JavaScript files for better speed

Google's Core Web Vitals favor fast websites—use caching & image optimization!

Final Thoughts

Great job! You've now:
- **Chosen a fast, SEO-friendly WordPress theme**
- **Customized your site's logo, colors, and fonts**
- **Installed essential plugins for security & performance**

Chapter 6: Creating Essential Website Pages

A successful website needs more than just great design—it must have **essential pages** that improve **SEO, user experience, and credibility**.

In this chapter, we'll cover:
- How to **design an engaging homepage**
- Writing a **compelling About page**
- Setting up a **Contact page with forms & Google Maps**
- Creating a **blog for SEO & audience engagement**
- Adding **Privacy Policy & Terms of Service** pages

Let's get started!

6.1 Homepage: Designing an Engaging First Impression

Your homepage is **the first thing visitors see**—it should be **clear, attractive, and optimized for conversions**.

Key Elements of a High-Converting Homepage

- **Clear Headline** – Describe what your website is about in **one sentence**.
- **Call-to-Action (CTA)** – Guide visitors with buttons like **"Get Started"** or **"Learn More"**.
- **Fast Loading Speed** – Keep images optimized for **fast performance**.

- **Mobile-Friendly Design** – Ensure your site looks great on **smartphones & tablets**.
- **SEO Optimized** – Include keywords in **headings & meta descriptions**.

Example Homepage Layout

[Header] – Logo + Navigation Menu
[Hero Section] – Headline + CTA Button
[Benefits] – Why choose you? (3 key points)
[Testimonials] – Social proof for credibility
[Final CTA] – Encourage visitors to take action

 SEO Tip: Use **H1 for the main heading** and **H2 for subheadings**.

6.2 About Page: Telling Your Story

The About page builds **trust** and **credibility** by sharing your story, mission, and values.

How to Write a Great About Page

. **Start with a strong opening** – Briefly explain **who you are & what you do**.
. **Share your story** – How did your business or blog start?
. **Highlight your mission** – What problem do you solve?
. **Include social proof** – Awards, testimonials, or case studies.
. **End with a CTA** – Guide visitors to explore your content or services.

Pro Tip: Add **a high-quality personal/team photo** to make the page more relatable!

6.3 Contact Page: Making It Easy to Connect

A Contact page allows visitors to **reach out quickly**. It should be **simple, clear, and functional**.

What to Include on Your Contact Page

- **Contact Form** – Visitors can send messages without opening email apps.
- **Email Address** – Provide an alternative way to contact you.
- **Google Maps** – Helps visitors **find your location** (if applicable).
- **Social Media Links** – Let users follow and engage with you.
- **Live Chat (Optional)** – A chat widget improves response time.

How to Add a Contact Form in WordPress

. Install the **WPForms** or **Contact Form 7** plugin.
. Create a new form and add fields like **Name, Email, Message**.
. Embed the form on your Contact page using a **shortcode**.

Bonus: If you have a **physical location**, embed **Google Maps** using the Google Maps plugin.

6.4 Blog Page: Driving Traffic with Content

A blog **improves SEO**, attracts visitors, and positions you as an expert.

How to Set Up a Blog in WordPress

1**Go to: Settings → Reading**
2-**Choose "Your latest posts"** as the homepage (for blogs)
3-**Create a Blog Page**

- **Go to: Pages → Add New**
- Title it **"Blog"** and publish
- Assign it as your Blog Page in **Settings → Reading**

Best Practices for SEO-Optimized Blog Posts

- **Write valuable content** – Answer common questions in your niche.
- **Use headings properly** – **H1 for titles, H2 for subtopics, H3 for details**.
- **Optimize images** – Compress images using **Smush** or **ShortPixel**.
- **Use internal linking** – Link to your other pages for **better navigation & SEO**.
- **Add meta descriptions** – Use **Yoast SEO** or **Rank Math** to optimize your posts.

 Tip: Aim for **at least one blog post per week** to keep your site active.

6.5 Privacy Policy & Terms of Service Pages

These pages are essential for **legal compliance** and **building trust**.

Why Are Legal Pages Important?

Required by law – GDPR, CCPA, and other regulations.
Protects your business – Defines user rights and limitations.
Improves credibility – Visitors trust websites with transparent policies.

How to Generate Privacy & Terms Pages

1 **Use a WordPress plugin** – Install **WP AutoTerms** for automatic legal pages.
2- **Use free generators** – Websites like **Termly or PrivacyPolicies.com** create custom policies.
3- **Customize for your website** – Include details about **data collection, cookies, and third-party services.**

Bonus: Add a **cookie consent banner** for GDPR compliance using the **Complianz plugin**.

Final Thoughts

Congratulations! You've now:
- **Created essential website pages** for SEO and user experience.
- **Designed a homepage** that converts visitors.
- **Set up a blog** to drive traffic.
- **Added legal pages** for compliance.

Chapter 7: Optimizing Website Performance and Security

A fast and secure website is **crucial for user experience and SEO**. Google ranks **fast-loading, secure** websites higher in search results, and visitors trust **safe** sites more.

In this chapter, you'll learn how to:
- **Improve website speed** (faster loading = better SEO!)
- **Enhance security** (protect against hackers & malware)
- **Set up regular backups** (prevent data loss)

Let's make your website **fast, secure, and reliable!**

7.1 Improving Website Speed

A **slow website** frustrates visitors and leads to **higher bounce rates**. Google also prioritizes **fast sites** in search rankings.

Key Strategies to Speed Up Your Website

- **Optimize Images** – Compress images to reduce file sizes
- **Enable Caching** – Store static content to load pages faster
- **Use a CDN (Content Delivery Network)** – Deliver content globally for speed

Image Optimization for Faster Loading

Large images **slow down** your website. **Optimize them** without losing quality.

. **Best Image Optimization Plugins (WordPress)**

Smush – Compress images automatically
ShortPixel – Reduces image sizes while keeping high quality
TinyPNG – Compress PNG/JPG images

Pro Tip: Use **WebP format** for even better speed!

Enabling Caching for Instant Loading

Caching **stores website data** so visitors don't have to reload everything every time.

. **Best Caching Plugins (WordPress)**

WP Rocket – Best premium caching plugin
LiteSpeed Cache – Ideal for Hostinger's LiteSpeed servers
W3 Total Cache – Advanced settings for performance

Pro Tip: If you're using **Hostinger**, enable **LiteSpeed Cache** from **hPanel → Performance Settings**!

Using a CDN (Content Delivery Network) for Global Speed

A **CDN (Cloudflare, BunnyCDN, etc.)** stores your website's data in multiple locations worldwide. When someone visits, the **nearest server** delivers the content = **super fast loading**!

. **How to Enable Cloudflare CDN in Hostinger**

1Go to **hPanel** → **Cloudflare**
2-Click **Enable Cloudflare**
3-Your website is now using Cloudflare's **fast global network**!

 Pro Tip: Cloudflare also improves **security** by blocking bad traffic.

7.2 Enhancing Website Security

Security is **critical** to protect your site from hackers, malware, and data breaches.

Essential Security Measures

- **Enable SSL (HTTPS) for data encryption**
- **Use Two-Factor Authentication (2FA) for login security**
- **Install security plugins to block malware & hackers**

Enabling SSL Certificate (HTTPS)

. SSL (Secure Sockets Layer) **encrypts data** and ensures a **secure connection**.
. Google **requires HTTPS** for ranking (non-HTTPS sites show a **"Not Secure" warning**).

. **How to Enable SSL in Hostinger**

1Go to **hPanel** → **SSL**
2-Click **Activate SSL Certificate**
3-Your site now has **HTTPS encryption** -

 Pro Tip: Install **Really Simple SSL** plugin for automatic HTTPS redirects.

Implementing Two-Factor Authentication (2FA)

2FA adds an extra **security layer** by requiring a **verification code** when logging in.

. How to Enable 2FA in WordPress

1Install **WP 2FA** or **Google Authenticator** plugin
2-Link to an authentication app (Google Authenticator, Authy)
3-Now, hackers **can't access your site** even if they steal your password!

 Pro Tip: Use **strong passwords** and limit login attempts with **Limit Login Attempts Reloaded**.

7.3 Regular Website Backups

Backups are **crucial** in case of data loss, hacking, or accidental errors.

Why Backups Are Essential

Protection against hacks – Restore your site instantly
Recovery from mistakes – Undo errors
Peace of mind – Never lose important data

Setting Up Automatic Backups on Hostinger

Hostinger offers **automated backups** to keep your website safe.

. How to Enable Automatic Backups in Hostinger

1Go to hPanel → **Backups**
2-Click **Enable Automatic Backups**
3-Choose **daily or weekly** backups

Your site is now **automatically backed up**! -

Restoring a Website from a Backup

If something goes wrong, you can **restore** your site in minutes.

. How to Restore a Backup in Hostinger

1Go to hPanel → **Backups**
2-Click **Restore** next to the backup date
3-Confirm restoration – Your website is back!

Pro Tip: Download **manual backups** for extra security.

Final Thoughts

Congratulations! You've now:
- **Optimized your website's speed** for faster loading
- **Enhanced security** with SSL & 2FA
- **Set up automatic backups** for data protection

Chapter 8: SEO Optimization for Higher Rankings

Want **more visitors** from Google?
SEO (**Search Engine Optimization**) is the **key** to **higher rankings, more traffic, and better conversions**.

In this chapter, you'll learn:
- **SEO Basics** – How search engines work
- **On-Page SEO** – Optimizing content, images, and metadata
- **Off-Page SEO** – Building backlinks and using social media

Let's **boost your website's visibility** and rank **higher on Google!**

8.1 Understanding SEO Basics

SEO is divided into **two main categories**:

. On-Page SEO (Optimizing Your Website Itself)

Optimizing **content, images, and headings**
Using **keywords** effectively
Improving **site speed & user experience**

. Off-Page SEO (Building Authority Outside Your Website)

Getting **backlinks** from other websites
Social media **engagement & shares**
Brand mentions & online reputation

Importance of Keyword Research

Choosing the **right keywords** helps Google understand your content and rank your website.

. Best Free Keyword Research Tools

Google Keyword Planner – Free keyword ideas
Ubersuggest – Find SEO difficulty & search volume
AnswerThePublic – Discover trending questions

Pro Tip: Use **long-tail keywords** (e.g., "best WordPress hosting for beginners") for **higher conversions** and less **competition**.

8.2 On-Page SEO Techniques

On-page SEO improves your website's **content, structure, and user experience**.

1Writing SEO-Friendly Content

Use Keywords Naturally – Avoid keyword stuffing
Write for Humans First, Google Second
Use Short Sentences & Paragraphs – Improves readability
Include Bullet Points & Lists – Makes content easy to scan

Pro Tip: Google **prefers longer, detailed articles** (1,500+ words) for ranking!

2-Using Meta Titles & Descriptions

Meta **titles & descriptions** appear in **Google search results**.

. Best Practices for Meta Titles

Include Keywords (Example: "Best WordPress Hosting – Hostinger Review")
Keep It Under 60 Characters
Make It Engaging – Encourage clicks!

. Best Practices for Meta Descriptions

Use Keywords Naturally
Keep It Under 160 Characters
Add a Call-to-Action (CTA) (Example: "Read our guide to get started today!")

Pro Tip: Use **Yoast SEO** or **Rank Math** to preview and optimize meta titles/descriptions in WordPress!

3-Optimizing Images for SEO

Large images **slow down your site** and hurt SEO.

. Best Image SEO Practices

Compress Images (Use **TinyPNG, Smush, or ShortPixel**)
Use Descriptive File Names (Example: `wordpress-hosting-guide.jpg` instead of `image123.jpg`)
Add Alt Text – Helps Google understand the image & improves accessibility

Pro Tip: Use **WebP format** instead of PNG/JPG for **faster loading**.

8.3 Off-Page SEO Strategies

Off-page SEO builds your **website authority & credibility**.

1Building High-Quality Backlinks

Backlinks (**links from other websites to yours**) **boost rankings**.

. Best Ways to Get Backlinks

Guest Posting – Write articles for other blogs & link back
Broken Link Building – Find broken links on other sites &
suggest your content as a replacement
HARO (Help A Reporter Out) – Get featured in news articles &
blogs

Pro Tip: Focus on **quality over quantity – One backlink from a
high-authority site (like Forbes) is better than 100 low-quality
links!**

2-Social Media Marketing for SEO

Google considers **social signals** (likes, shares, comments) as
indicators of quality.

. Best Social Media Strategies for SEO

Share Blog Posts Regularly (on Facebook, Twitter, LinkedIn)
Engage With Followers – More interactions = more visibility
Use Hashtags – Helps reach a bigger audience

Pro Tip: Pinterest is **great** for driving **long-term SEO traffic** to
your site!

Final Thoughts

Congratulations! You've now:
- Learned **SEO basics**
- Optimized **your website for Google rankings**
- Built **backlinks & social engagement**

Chapter 9: Launching and Maintaining Your Website

Congratulations! Your website is almost **ready to go live.** But before launching, you need to:
- **Check website performance & speed**
- **Optimize for mobile & SEO**
- **Promote your website for traffic growth**
- **Maintain & update regularly for long-term success**

Let's walk through **everything you need** to launch & maintain a successful website!

9.1 Final Website Checklist Before Launch

Before you hit **"Publish"**, make sure your website is **optimized for performance, security, and user experience**.

Testing Website Responsiveness (Mobile-Friendly Design)

More than **60% of internet users** browse on **mobile devices**. Ensure your site:
- **Loads properly on all screen sizes** (Use Google's Mobile-Friendly Test)
- **Has easy-to-click buttons** and **readable fonts**
- **Uses a mobile-responsive theme**

 Pro Tip: Use the **Google Chrome DevTools (F12 → Toggle Device Toolbar)** to preview your site on **mobile, tablet, and desktop**.

Ensuring Website Speed Optimization

Fast-loading websites:
 Rank higher on Google
 Reduce bounce rates
 Provide a better user experience

. **Speed Optimization Checklist:**

- **Use a lightweight theme** (e.g., Astra, GeneratePress)
- **Enable caching** (Use WP Rocket or LiteSpeed Cache)
- **Optimize images** (Use WebP format + ShortPixel)
- **Use a Content Delivery Network (CDN)** (Cloudflare speeds up your site)

Pro Tip: Test your website speed with **Google PageSpeed Insights** or **GTmetrix** before launch. Aim for **under 3 seconds** load time!

9.2 Promoting Your Website

Now that your website is live, you need **visitors**! Here's how to drive traffic:

1-Social Media Marketing Strategies

Share your content on social media (Facebook, Twitter, LinkedIn, Pinterest)
Join niche-specific groups & communities (e.g., Facebook Groups, Reddit)
Use engaging visuals (Canva helps create eye-catching images)
Leverage Pinterest (Great for long-term website traffic)

Pro Tip: Create **short-form videos** on **Instagram Reels, TikTok, and YouTube Shorts** to drive more engagement!

2-Email Marketing Basics

Email marketing is one of the **best ways** to keep visitors coming back.

. **How to Start Email Marketing:**

- **Set up a free email list** (Use Mailchimp, ConvertKit, or Brevo)
- **Offer a freebie (lead magnet)** – Example: "Get a Free SEO Checklist"
- **Send valuable emails** – Tips, blog updates, exclusive content

 Pro Tip: Create an **exit-intent pop-up** (via OptinMonster) to capture more emails before users leave!

9.3 Ongoing Maintenance and Updates

To keep your website **secure, updated, and ranking on Google**, follow these steps:

1Regular Content Updates

Google **loves fresh content**! Keep your website active by:
- **Publishing new blog posts** regularly
- **Updating old content** with new data & keywords
- **Adding internal links** to keep users engaged

 Pro Tip: Refresh old content every **6 months** to keep rankings high!

2-Monitoring Website Performance with Google Analytics

Google Analytics helps you track:
Traffic sources – Where visitors come from
User behavior – What pages they visit most
Bounce rate – If users leave too soon

. How to Set Up Google Analytics:

- **Go to Google Analytics**
- **Set up a new property** for your website
- **Install the tracking code** (via Google Tag Manager or a plugin like Site Kit)

 Pro Tip: Also set up **Google Search Console** to track **SEO performance & keyword rankings**.

Final Thoughts

 Your website is now live! You've:
- Tested & optimized for speed
- Promoted on social media & email
- Set up analytics for growth

Conclusion: Your Website Journey Begins!

Congratulations! You've successfully learned **how to create, launch, and optimize a website using Hostinger**. Whether you're building a blog, e-commerce store, or portfolio, you now have the essential tools and knowledge to make your site **fast, secure, and SEO-friendly**.

But remember—**website success is an ongoing journey**! Keep optimizing, updating content, and experimenting with different strategies to **grow your audience and increase traffic**.

Next Steps: Keep Improving Your Website

. **Monitor website performance** with Google Analytics
. **Update old content** to keep rankings high
. **Explore monetization strategies** (ads, affiliate marketing, e-commerce)
. **Stay updated with SEO trends** (Google algorithm updates change frequently)

Pro Tip: Bookmark this guide and revisit it whenever you need to tweak or improve your site!

Bonus: Free Resources

. Must-Have Free SEO Tools

- **Google Search Console** – Track your website's SEO performance
- **Google PageSpeed Insights** – Check website speed & fix performance issues
- **Ubersuggest** – Free keyword research tool
- **AnswerThePublic** – Discover trending content ideas
- **GTmetrix** – Analyze and improve website loading speed
- **Rank Math / Yoast SEO** – WordPress plugins for SEO optimization

---

. Recommended Online Courses for Website Building

📌 **Hostinger Tutorials** – Official guides on web hosting & WordPress
📌 **Google Digital Garage** – Free course on digital marketing & SEO
📌 **Coursera – WordPress for Beginners** – Learn how to build WordPress sites step by step
📌 **HubSpot Academy – SEO Training** – Free SEO course to

improve rankings

📌 <u>**Udemy – WordPress & Website Development**</u> – Affordable courses on website creation

Final Words: Keep Learning & Growing!

Your website is now **live and optimized**, but the journey doesn't end here! Keep improving, learning, and experimenting with new strategies to **boost traffic, engagement, and revenue**.

. Need help? **Join online communities** (Facebook Groups, Reddit forums, etc.)
. Stay updated on **SEO trends** to maintain high rankings
. Don't forget to **back up your site regularly** to avoid data loss

Your website is your digital asset—keep growing it, and success will follow!

Table of Contents :

www.ingramcontent.com/pod-product-compliance
Lightning Source LLC
LaVergne TN
LVHW051618050326
832903LV00033B/4561